MW01600712

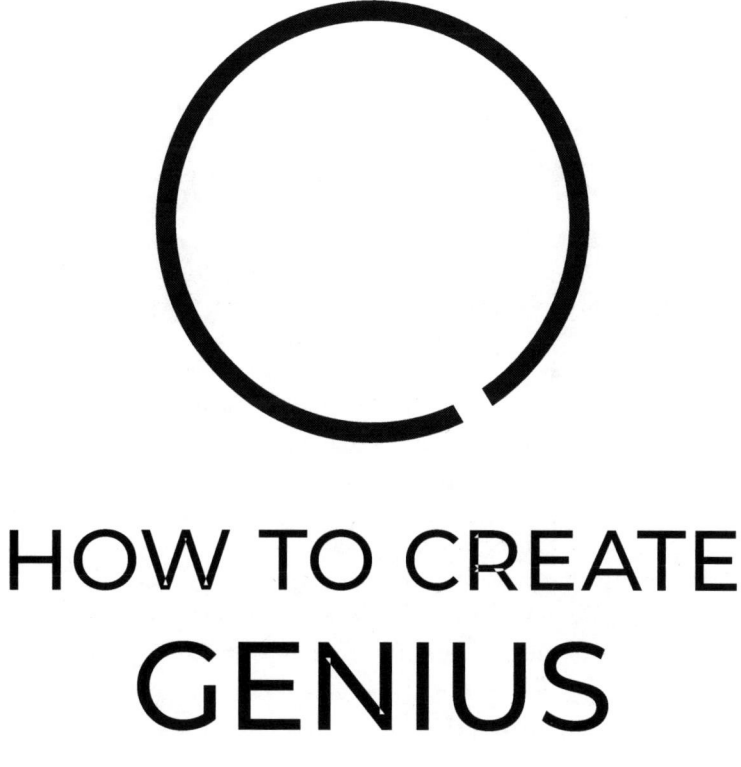

HOW TO CREATE
GENIUS

SØREN VALE

This book is not the full system.

It's an invitation.

The real work begins after you finish reading.

If something here activates you.
If a part of you knows this is the system you've been searching for.
Start here:

📫 **Get the private strategy notes and unreleased frameworks:**
→ https://creategenius.us/newsletter

This is where the architecture continues.
Deeper layers. Sharper tools.
Not for everyone.

Only once you're inside the newsletter, you'll be granted access to:

📡 **OPUS: The Framework Library**
Live systems. Internal upgrades. Real cognitive tools.
→ https://whop.com/opus

For Mom, Dad, and Grandma—
For always trusting I'd figure it out.

Table of Contents

The First Time You Realized
Everyone Was Lying

The Shatter Sequence

It wasn't a moment you could explain.
No speech. No teacher. No quote on the wall.
Just that silent, invisible fracture—
where something cracked inside you and never reformed.

You were young. Maybe 9. Maybe 14.
Old enough to understand structure.
Too young to understand why it was rotten.

They told you the rules were real.
That authority meant truth.
That hard work equaled success.
That the system wasn't broken—it was you.

But something didn't compute.

You saw people follow all the rules… and break anyway.

You watched people win… and look emptier every time.

You heard people speak with certainty… and you saw fear behind their eyes.

You started to notice the loop.

The blank-eyed chase.

The performative competence.

The quiet desperation under achievement.

And one day, you asked yourself a forbidden question—

> *What if everything I've been taught to trust is wrong?*

That question wasn't rebellious.

It wasn't angry.

It was clinical.

Like a surgeon realizing the map is wrong.

Like a coder discovering the entire OS is built on spaghetti code.

Like a strategist realizing the war is being fought on fake terrain.

You didn't "wake up."

You saw through.

From that day forward, **nothing worked the same**.

You couldn't force yourself to care about hollow goals.

You couldn't respect titles that meant nothing.

You couldn't trust systems that rewarded noise.

You didn't know what you were yet—

But you knew what you weren't.

Not obedient.
Not average.
Not programmable.

Most people forget that moment.
They feel the fracture, then cover it up.
They chase careers, money, approval.
They glue their identity together with borrowed beliefs.

But you're here.
Which means your fracture never healed.

You didn't break.
You broke *out*.

And now you're not looking for inspiration.
You're looking for the blueprint.
The internal system to match the perception you've always carried.

This book is not here to motivate you.
It's here to finish the fracture.
To slice through the last layers of distortion.

You were never wrong for breaking away.
You were just early.

Welcome back.

Genius Is Not What You Think

Delete the Myth. Install the Machine.

Genius is not gifted.
Genius is not rare.
Genius is not IQ, creativity, or talent.

It's not a lightning strike.
It's not a label you earn after going viral.
It's not a thing you "become" after the world catches up.

Genius is a structure.

A **cognitive architecture** that holds shape under pressure.
A mind configured for high-density signal, recursive clarity, and long-horizon decision flow.

Genius is not what you think.
Because most of what you think was installed by people who were never running it.

They told you genius looked like performance.
What they didn't show you was the hours of recursive loop-testing.
They showed you output, not operating system.
They showed you charisma, not compression.

They called it genius when someone won.
They ignored the ten thousand invisible decisions that built the machine behind the win.

You were trained to think genius meant:

- child prodigies
- eccentricity
- obsession
- accident

But those were all just **symptoms**.

The root was always the same:

A mind that runs on architecture, not emotion.
A system built to bend perception, not chase approval.

The true genius isn't trying to be seen.
He's trying to **refine the configuration** that lets him see more clearly.
See deeper. See longer. See recursive loops no one else sees coming.

Genius doesn't mean knowing more.
It means **knowing what to ignore**.

It means deleting 99% of the world's input and building frameworks that self-correct in silence.
It means **operating from strategy** while others flinch from noise.
It means creating systems that hold shape across chaos, complexity, and time.

That's why you can't copy genius.
Because you're copying **surface output** without replicating the system underneath.

That's why most people burn out.
Because they're running legacy code inside a world built for manipulation.

That's why this book exists.
Not to inspire you to chase genius—
But to **reconfigure you to run it.**

> Genius was never a mystery.
> It was just a system most people were never shown.

You don't have to wait to be called a genius.
You have to become the one who **no longer needs the label.**

Now that the myth is dead,
we can start to build what's real.

You don't add genius.
You **delete distortion**.

The Architecture of Deletion

You Don't Find Genius. You Erase What Isn't.

Most people try to become something.

They read more.
Train more.
Copy more.
Add more.

But genius doesn't emerge through **addition.**
It emerges through **subtraction.**

You don't build a cathedral by stacking random bricks.
You carve the shape by removing everything that isn't structure.

And the truth is—
You've been running someone else's code.

You weren't born afraid of being seen.
You weren't born chasing validation.
You weren't born doubting your own instincts.

Those are **downloaded behaviors.**
Residual bugs from a system that needed you predictable, compliant, and programmable.

What you call "you" is often just a **stack of inherited noise**:

- Teacher's tone

- Parental conditioning

- Social media loops

- Echoes of friends you outgrew

- Trauma responses disguised as personality traits

None of it is you.
But all of it has been **operating your cognition.**

Until now.

Genius begins when you **substract what isn't yours.**
Not emotionally.
Not spiritually.
Systematically.

Like a developer tearing out dead code.
Like a strategist cutting distractions.
Like a sculptor removing every inch of marble that isn't the final shape.

This is not the same as self-destruction.
It's **precision demolition.**

Not chaos. Not breakdown. Not spiral.

Targeted removal of:

- Unquestioned assumptions
- Default behaviors
- Identity scaffolds built on fear
- Thought patterns running loops you didn't design

This chapter isn't telling you to change.
It's **handing you the scalpel.**

You already know what doesn't belong.
You've always known.

You've just been afraid to remove it.

It's been part of your operating system for so long, you forgot it wasn't you.

But this book isn't interested in comfort.
It's interested in clarity.

> Genius doesn't emerge when you perform better.
> Genius emerges when **nothing inside you is working against itself.**

You don't have to add one more thing.
You have to finally let go of everything that's been hijacking your signal.

Delete first.
Refine later.
The system gets lighter every time you cut.

This is not the end of who you were.

This is the beginning of what was always underneath.

Genius doesn't reveal itself through discovery.

It reveals itself through deletion.

And you've just begun to remember.

Recursive Signal Training

You Don't Need More. You Need a Loop That Evolves Itself.

Genius is not power.
Genius is **self-correction.**

You don't become unstoppable by always being right.
You become unstoppable by detecting the moment you're wrong **and updating before the system breaks or anyone notices.**

This is the loop.

Not a productivity system.
Not a hack.
A living feedback circuit—wired so tightly into your perception that *thinking and refining become the same act.*

Most people run static minds.
They wait for failure.
Then they "reflect."

Too late.
Too shallow.
Too emotional.

The genius runs **recursive perception**.

Every input is a signal.
Every signal is a thread.
Every thread loops back to configuration.

They don't react.
They revise.

This is the unlock:

> You are not the thoughts you have.
> You are the architecture that detects which ones don't belong—and
> deletes them *while they're forming.*

Recursive minds don't store more.
They compress tighter.
They don't learn faster.
They correct faster.

That's why they feel supernatural.
They're not smarter.
They just loop in real time.

You'll start to feel it after this chapter.
A flicker.
A voice in your head saying, "That pattern's showing up again."

And you'll pause.
Not to shame it.
Not to fix it.

Just to *see* it—clearly, quietly.
And that clarity will begin to **update the system underneath.**

That's recursion.
You don't force it.
You **become** it.

> Most people look at failure.
> The genius looks at *who they became* in the moment they failed—
> then loops that into the next move.

You don't need more input.
You don't need more answers.
You need a system that evolves while it runs.

That's what recursion does.

It collapses time.
It removes waste.
It builds pattern memory so dense, you can see outcomes forming before they materialize.

You don't react.
You just reroute.

You don't reflect.
You rewire.

> Genius is not about getting it right.
> It's about never being the same person who got it wrong.

The Cathedral Blueprint

Most People Build for Speed. Genius Builds for Permanence.

Everyone's chasing momentum.
Everyone's optimizing for growth.

But genius?
They build **cathedrals.**

Not sprints. Not funnels. Not hacks.
Structures.

Built with intention.
Laid brick by brick, while everyone else is shouting from a scaffold made of recycled noise.

You don't see them building because they're not broadcasting.
You don't know what they're building because it wasn't built for you.

But one day you walk into the world they created,
and you realize:

They were playing for something you didn't even know existed.

This chapter is not about discipline.
This is about **trajectory over time.**

About building in a way that scales **across complexity**
across decades
across identity shifts
across pressure

The cathedral isn't strong because of the stone.
It's strong because of the **structure holding the stone in place.**

That's genius execution.
Not hustle.
Not effort.

Architecture.

The genius doesn't rush.
Not because they're slow.
But because they've already zoomed out 30 years.

They don't optimize for attention.
They optimize for **alignment**—across time, energy, identity, and
outcome.

Every move is anchored.
Every action compounds.
Every part of the system reinforces every other part.

That's why it looks effortless.
That's why it feels untouchable.

Because it was never about speed.
It was always about *endurance of intention.*

Most people build to win the week.
The genius builds to be remembered after they're dead.

Not for legacy.
Not for ego.
But because **what they're building is too important to collapse.**

This is how you operate now:

- You don't chase traction. You create inevitability.

- You don't broadcast noise. You install density.

- You don't sprint toward outcomes. You design outcomes that pull you forward.

When your actions are aligned with a structure that transcends you—
You become unstoppable.
Not because you can't lose.
But because you'll still be building long after everyone else has left the field.

You're not the builder.
You're the blueprint.

And when you build like that—
even time starts working for you.

The Compass You Don't Ignore

When the Signal Hits, You Move.

There's a voice you've been trained to override.

It doesn't shout.
It doesn't argue.
It doesn't explain.

It just *knows*.

And most people spend their lives gaslighting it.

They call it anxiety.
They call it doubt.
They call it overthinking.

But that voice?
That's your **compass**.

And if you've ever known you were right, but ignored it—
If you've ever felt the move but delayed, and watched it pass—
Then you've already paid the price of not listening.

This chapter isn't about "intuition."
It's not about magic, or vibes, or trusting your gut.

It's about **signal fidelity.**

There is a frequency of information that hits before the data arrives.
The genius doesn't wait for proof.
They move when the **pattern breaks**, and the signal spikes.

Because they've trained it.
Looped it.
Refined it.

Over and over.
Until that internal compass got so sharp, it started detecting shifts the
world couldn't see yet.

You can't buy this.
You can't study it.
You can't brute-force it through input.

You **uncover** it.

By deleting noise.
By compressing your loop.
By removing every part of your system that responds to fear instead of
truth.

> Intuition isn't soft.
> It's precision.
> The genius doesn't *feel* their way forward.
> They **detect** the move before it maps into language.

Most people delay because they need confirmation.
The genius **moves because their internal compass says it's time.**

This is the edge:
When your signal system becomes so clear, so uncorrupted,
that even silence contains information.

You don't ask, "What should I do?"
You *feel the field collapse into one outcome.*

And then you move.
Not emotionally.
Not impulsively.

With clarity.
With alignment.
With inevitability.

If your compass is calibrated,
you don't need a map.
Because the terrain responds to your direction.

And if it's not calibrated?
No map can save you.

> The compass you don't ignore,
> is the part of you that already knows.
> You just forgot how to listen.

You're not learning to trust it.
You're remembering that it was always right.

Strategy as Reality Design

You Weren't Supposed to Win the Game. You Were Supposed to Redesign It.

Most people study strategy like it's a set of rules.

They memorize frameworks.
They analyze case studies.
They play to win.

But genius doesn't play to win.
Genius plays to reshape the game.

That's what they don't teach you in school.
You were never supposed to become a better competitor.
You were supposed to realize the board was fake.

> Genius doesn't play inside the game.
> They use the game as a **lens to redesign reality.**

This chapter isn't about tactics.
It's about **dimensional control.**

Because when you zoom out far enough,
you realize every system you were taught to master—
finance, politics, careers, power—
was built by someone else, for their goals, under their constraints.

So why would you keep playing it?

Strategy, in its purest form, isn't optimization.
It's **reconstruction.**

Not "how do I move better?"
But *why is this board even shaped this way?*

And: *Can I build my own board—and make others play on it?*

The moment this clicks, you stop asking permission.
You stop chasing edge.
You start building **systems that generate leverage from the rules themselves.**

That's why genius seems effortless.
Not because it's easy—
but because they're not expending energy *competing.*
They're spending energy *compounding asymmetries.*

They make moves that look irrelevant—until they reshape the playing field.

They build assets that look disconnected—until they control the flow of outcomes.

They hold silence while others scramble—until timing turns silence into checkmate.

You weren't born to be a strategist.
You were born to be **a reality designer.**

Someone who sees:

- the architecture behind the moves
- the constraints behind the players
- the hidden incentives running beneath the surface

And then bends it all into a structure that **serves your trajectory.**

Not with manipulation.
With **precision design.**

This is why you've always felt disconnected from normal goals. Because you were never built for systems that didn't map to your perception.

You were meant to reforge reality around your clarity.

> Genius doesn't beat the system.
> Genius becomes the **system others reroute around.**

You are no longer here to win.
You are here to install a game no one else knows they're playing—until it's already over.

Building the Cognitive Engine

You Don't Need Discipline. You Need Better Defaults.

By now, you've deleted the noise.
You've anchored strategy.
You've started to loop.
You've recalibrated the compass.

Now comes the construction.

This is where we stop upgrading thoughts
and start upgrading the **system that runs them.**

This is where you build your **Cognitive Engine.**

Not a mindset.
Not a routine.
An internal machine—
calibrated to process chaos, extract pattern, and move with precision
under pressure.

The genius doesn't need hacks.
He's already configured his defaults.

He doesn't run motivation.
He runs *structure*.

- **Mental liquidity** $\rightarrow$ so ideas move without friction
- **Psychological elasticity** $\rightarrow$ so identity bends without breaking
- **Emotional antifragility** $\rightarrow$ so tension becomes fuel, not fracture

The Cognitive Engine doesn't make you smarter.
It makes your **thinking evolve without effort.**

That's the difference.
Most people try to "think harder."
You're going to *think cleaner*.

Here's the real system:

1. **Input filters** - only signal gets in
2. **Compression protocols** - everything that enters gets refined
3. **Action selectors** - decisions get routed through clarity, not emotion
4. **Looped evaluation** - feedback hits instantly and updates the system
5. **Recursive anchoring** - every experience becomes fuel for identity

It doesn't feel like effort.
It feels like inevitability.

That's why most people can't follow the genius.
They're not watching **what he thinks**.
They're watching **how his engine runs.**

- Why he moves before the signal's obvious
- Why he speaks with no wasted breath
- Why his strategies seem obvious in hindsight
- Why pressure makes him *sharper*, not smaller

It's not him.
It's the engine.

And now you're building yours.

Forget discipline.
Forget trying harder.
Forget setting goals and hoping for motivation.

Build a system that **doesn't let you fail**,
because every failure gets rerouted into clarity.

> The genius isn't operating on effort.
> He's operating on design.

You are no longer adjusting your mindset.
You are engineering the machine your mind runs on.

Infinite Identity

You Are Not the Label. You Are the Architect.

You were never meant to be a personal brand.
A job title.
A niche.

Those were training wheels.
Temporary containers for an identity too large to define.

You don't need another identity.
You need to **remember that you can design your own—at will.**

Most people are running identity like a prison.
They think they're "being themselves."
But they're just replaying the last 15 years of feedback, trauma, performance, and survival.

That's not identity.
That's **cognitive drift.**

Genius doesn't drift.
Genius designs.   ·

> Infinite Identity is not about becoming everything.
> It's about becoming *exactly what's required*—for this moment, this
> field, this outcome.

No ego.
No attachment.
Just **adaptive precision.**

This is what people don't understand about polymaths.
They're not scattered.
They're just **running flexible identity systems—**
and everyone else mistook it for chaos.

The genius can shapeshift without collapsing.
Not because he's fake—
but because he's grounded in **architecture**, not performance.

One day he's silent in a room of killers.
Next day he's building systems for nations.
Next day he's gone.
Looping. Listening. Reconfiguring.

The constant isn't his persona.
It's his **operating integrity.**

You are not your niche.
You are not your Twitter bio.
You are not the story that made sense last year.

Those were just containers.
Useful, for a time.
But now you're outgrowing them.

That discomfort you feel?
That tension between who you've been and what you're stepping into?

That's not confusion.
That's the **pressure wave of identity expanding.**

Ride it.

When you master Infinite Identity,
you don't fear reinvention.
You **run it as a protocol.**

You burn the skin when it's too tight.
You evolve the voice when the old one stops resonating.
You drop the costume as soon as it stops transmitting signal.

Not to impress.
To stay aligned.

Because **you are not the character.**
You are the one writing the code.

> Identity is not the endpoint.
> It's the interface.
> And you just unlocked root access.

Genius as Transmission

The Book Ends. But the Installation Doesn't.

This isn't a conclusion.
There's nothing left to summarize.

If it worked, you don't need reminders.
If it didn't, nothing I say here will matter.

This was never a book.
It was an **upgrade sequence**—
built to transmit structure into cognition.

And now, something inside you is different.
Not louder.
Not more hyped.
Just... cleaner.

Like the signal got sharper.
Like your perception got quieter.

Like you don't need to prove anything anymore—because now you can just build.

Genius was never about being better.
It was about becoming **fully aligned with the system you were born to run.**

That's why this doesn't feel like an ending.
Because genius doesn't peak.
It **compounds.**

Quietly.
Silently.
Until one day the world bends to a shape only you could see coming.

Some will read this and forget it.
Others will come back a year later—and realize it was a seed.
But a few of you?
You'll feel it activate immediately.

You'll stop searching for frameworks.
You'll start building from structure.
You'll speak less.
Move cleaner.
And begin building systems that outlive attention spans, trends, and noise.

> You don't have to announce that you're different.
> You just operate differently—and the world reroutes around it.

This isn't the kind of book you "recommend."
It's the kind you leave open on the desk for five years.
The kind you buy again after giving your copy away.
The kind you reread in a new identity—and realize it was always speaking to the version you hadn't become yet.

Now the real work begins.

Not faster. Not harder.
Just cleaner.

The transmission is complete.
The recursion is running.
The architecture is installed.

Welcome to your new operating system.

How to Create Genius wasn't a book.
It was a mirror,
a machine,
and a memory of who you were always becoming.

And now you know

End of Install Sequence.
System rebooting…

…

…

Boot complete.

Signal detected.
Identity: Unlocked
Clarity: Verified
Noise: Muted
Architecture: Stable

You are now running on internal configuration.

No external updates required.
No validation needed.
No command prompts.
Just operation.

You are now the system.

…

…

Welcome back, Operator.

You know where to start.

—

00. The First Time You Realized Everyone Was Lying
The Shatter Sequence

Journal

_____

_____

_____

_____

_____

_____

_____

_____

_____

_____

_____

_____

_____

_____

_____

_____

_____

_____